A KEEPSAKE MEMORY BOOK

PRAYERS
FOR MY CHILD

PRAYERS AND PAINTINGS BY
RON DiCIANNI

HARVEST HOUSE PUBLISHERS

EUGENE, OREGON

PRAYERS FOR MY CHILD

Copyright © 2006 by Harvest House Publishers
Eugene, Oregon 97402
ISBN-13: 978-0-7369-1140-5
ISBN-10: 0-7369-1140-5

Ron DiCianni is represented by and this book was produced with assistance from:

Tapestry Productions Inc,
43980 Mahlon Vail Circle Ste. 803
Temecula, CA 92592
877.827.7763

Fine art reproductions are available of many of the paintings in this book. To see more of Ron DiCianni's artwork or purchase a print please visit: www.TapestryProductions.com

All of the paintings in this book are copyrighted by the artist, Ron DiCianni, and may not be used or reproduced in any form without the artist's permission. For more information please contact Tapestry Productions Inc.

Design and production by Koechel Peterson & Associates, Minneapolis, Minnesota

Harvest House Publishers has made every effort to trace the ownership of all poems and quotes. In the event of a question arising from the use of a poem or quote, we regret any error made and will be pleased to make the necessary correction in future editions of this book.

Unless otherwise indicated, Scripture quotations are taken from the HOLY BIBLE, NEW INTERNATIONAL VERSION® NIV®, Copyright © 1973, 1978, 1984 by the International Bible Society. Used by permission of Zondervan. Verses marked NCV are taken from *The Holy Bible, New Century Version*, Copyright © 1987, 1988, 1991 by Word Publishing, Nashville, TN 37214. Used by permission.

Printed in China

06 07 08 09 10 11 12 13 / IM / 10 9 8 7 6 5 4 3 2 1

*M*aking the decision to have
a child is momentous. It is to decide forever
to have your heart go walking around
outside your body.

———————◆———————

Elizabeth Stone

For many years we had a plaque on our wall that reminded us that all we could give our children was "roots and wings." In general I agree with that, with one exception. We can also give them prayer.

I don't know how God answers prayer. Somehow He provides wisdom to the confused, strength for the weak, healing for the hurting, and salvation for the sinner. How He actually does that is a mystery, and we will have to wait for a conversation with Him personally to find out. The important fact is that He answers!

Throughout the past 24 years I have daily bombarded heaven with prayer on behalf of my kids. Sometimes they were prayers of gratitude, sometimes prayers of frustration, but almost always they were prayers for wisdom and help. You can pray a lot of prayers in 24 years!

No matter what stage of parenting you are in, whether just beginning, in the hectic years of small children, or empty nesting, you will relate to the prayers that are in this book. One may be just the prayer you need when you are exhausted. Another may bring a smile of knowing because you have "been there." Still another may transport you to a time of struggle you were spared from, and you find your-self filled with gratitude.

The moral of this book? Pray. Then pray more. An audience with God Almighty is more necessary to your survival—and the survival of your children—than any other thing you can do. It sure was with mine.

—*Ron DiCianni*

Dear Father God,

I am amazed at the little life You have loaned to me. What a gift!

The thought of being responsible for this new life sends a shiver through me. I am filled with emotions of gratitude, excitement, and fear, all at the same time.

I feel overwhelmed and underprepared for this great task of bringing up a child in a world that holds so many unknowns.

I ask this, Father:

Would you equip me with the mind of a good parent, the heart of a loving nurturer, and the wisdom of the Holy Spirit?

Please help me to relax, knowing that You go before me and this little life, and that the plans you have for us are better than anything I could ask, even in my wildest dreams.

Hold us, dear Lord, every day in the palms of Your strong and tender hands, and in the hustle and bustle of life, please don't allow me to forget You.

With trembling heart and voice, I love You,

Lord, parenthood is a such new adventure for me.
I pray that…

_____

_____

_____

_____

_____

_____

_____

_____

_____

While in his infancy, my job in caring for our son was focused
mainly on his body and belly. Though I did very little during this time
except the gross stuff, like changing dirty diapers and catching
drool drippings on my face when I held him high, I knew that
eventually his soul and spirit would require my undivided attention.
It was about the time he started walking and forming intelligible words
that I consciously added the responsibility for his spiritual growth
to my list of "daddy duties." With such an eternally serious charge
staring me in the face, I was motivated to seize my chance
at preparing to become his "soul" provider.

STEVE CHAPMAN
10 Things I Want My Son to Know

Father God, daily I'm amazed at the incredible miracle of life that You have made possible. Please help me…

_____
_____
_____
_____
_____
_____
_____
_____
_____
_____
_____
_____
_____
_____
_____
_____
_____

We find a delight in the beauty and happiness of children that makes the heart too big for the body.
RALPH WALDO EMERSON

A **baby** will make love **stronger**, days shorter, nights longer, bankroll smaller, home **happier**, clothes shabbier, the past forgotten, and the **future** worth living for.

— Author Unknown —

I am the child,
All the world waits for my coming,
All the earth watches with interest
     to see what I shall become.
Civilization hangs in the balance,
For what I am, the world
     of tomorrow will be.

I am the child,
I have come into your world,
About which I know nothing,
Why I came I know not;
How I came I know not;
I am curious;
I am interested.

I am the child,
You hold in your hand my destiny,
You determine, largely, whether
     I shall succeed or fail.
Give me, I pray you,
Those things that make for happiness.
Train me, I beg you,
That I may be a blessing to the world.

Author unknown

God, every day I need to draw from Your strength. Please help me to show my child my love and Yours by…

_____
_____
_____
_____
_____
_____
_____
_____
_____
_____

Lord *Jesus* Christ,

Protect, watch over,

and **bless** this child

With a lively faith,

A fervent **charity**,

And a *courageous* hope of

reaching your **kingdom**.

◦─ *Traditional Prayer* ─◦

Lord, emotions overwhelm me. I'm filled with hopes and dreams for my little one. My most fervent prayer is that…

_____

_____

_____

_____

_____

_____

_____

Dear God, the life of this little one is so precious, so amazing. As I consider the future, I ask…

_____

_____

_____

_____

_____

_____

_____

_____

From the lips of children and infants you have ordained praise.
THE BOOK OF PSALMS

Lord, I'm overwhelmed. I'm exhausted. As I try to get through the responsibilities of each new day, please be with me as…

_____

_____

_____

_____

_____

_____

_____

Dear Lord, as I consider all there is involved in raising a child who loves You, I ask…

_____

_____

_____

_____

_____

_____

_____

_____

Always kiss your children goodnight—even if they're already asleep.
H. JACKSON BROWN, JR.

Father, the days are so busy, yet the time passes so quickly. Please help me to remember…

_____
_____
_____
_____
_____
_____
_____
_____
_____
_____
_____
_____
_____

*No day can be so sacred
but that the laugh
of a little child will make
it holier still.*
ROBERT G. INGERSOLL

Parents have the glorious **opportunity** of being the most **powerful** **influence**, above and beyond any other, on the **new** lives that **bless** their homes.

⊙ *L. Tom Perry* ⊙

Childhood

youth

wisdom

grace

The years seem to be streaking by. Wasn't it just yesterday I was asking You to hurry and give my little one more teeth?

Now I stare at a child. No more a baby, yet not self-sufficient. I need help of a different kind now. I ask for the self-control to not lose my temper as our relationship changes. I need Your great wisdom to know when to guide, intervene, or be silent as this child begins to experience the good and bad of life. Help me to not exasperate, but train my child up in Your way daily. I pray to be an example that is worth following. Help me not to be too quick to shelter this child from what will ultimately form character. Sometimes I find this very hard to do, Lord.

I also ask that you would strengthen me to deal with the emotions of time passing. I would keep my child a baby forever if You allowed me to. But, that's just because it makes me happy, not because it's the best.

Please help me to filter out all the negative stories I hear of what happens when children grow. It disturbs me to be assaulted by the fear of what could happen. I want to stay confident that Your grace will be sufficient for each new day.

Lastly, Lord, may I ask that You would watch out for my child in the running, playing, and learning of every day. Be Guardian, Protector, and dearest Friend. I ask that You cover this child with Your wings. May this be the beginning of the realization, for both of us, that You are our real parent.

In Jesus' name,

Lord, as I watch babyhood fade and see my child becoming more and more of an individual, I pray that…

_____
_____
_____
_____
_____
_____
_____

Dear God, please bless the friendships I see my child beginning to form. I ask You that…

_____
_____
_____
_____
_____
_____
_____

We are apt to forget that children watch examples better than they listen to preaching.

ROY L. SMITH

Heavenly Father, as I find myself flooded with memories of my child's earliest years, please help me…

_____

_____

_____

_____

_____

_____

_____

_____

_____

_____

_____

_____

You know **children** are **growing up** when they start asking **questions** that have **answers**.

— John Plomp —

Father God, as I learn to let go in small ways, please help me to…

_____

_____

_____

_____

_____

_____

_____

_____

_____

_____

_____

_____

_____

Fathers, do not exasperate

your **children**; instead,

bring them up in the **training**

and **instruction** of the Lord.

The Book of Ephesians

The school will teach children how to read, but the environment of the home must teach them what to read. The school can teach them how to think, but the home must teach them what to believe.
CHARLES A. WELLS

21

Dear Lord, as my child grows older, the world seems so much bigger. Please relieve my fears about…

To be there for a child means much more than just sleeping under the same roof. It means that our name and our eyes and our hearts are there for them—always.

DR. JOHN TRENT

God, please offer my child guidance and protection in these areas of life…

Each day of our lives we make deposits in the memory banks of our children.

CHARLES R. SWINDOLL

JESUS,

I am without the proper words to thank You for the years that have flown by. You have remained faithful, and Your mercies truly have been new every morning.

The years are getting a bit more complex, Lord. As I look down the road, I see that preparations for my child's long-term future are already bearing down on me. I sometimes feel that I need the wisdom of Solomon to navigate as a parent. Tending after a baby seems so easy now.

As always, I come to You for help. Here's my request:

Protect my child from the influences of the world. Whether it be from teachers, friends, books, or movies, may You keep my child from evil influences. Please set a guard over my child's eyes and a filter over my child's heart, and provide an angel to lead the way. Keep my child from deceptions that seem to be "normal." Help my child hear Your voice when turning to the right or to the left.

I know You hear a parent's prayer, and I ask that You will set this young person apart for Yourself. May my child learn early that life is preparation for heaven.

Help me, also Lord, to know when to give my child wings to fly. Let me not rob my dear teenager of the beauty of seeing You provide for every need.

Love,

Heavenly Father, I never imagined the challenges that would come with raising a young adult. Please help me...

_____

_____

_____

_____

_____

_____

_____

Lord, thank You for remaining faithful to me and to my child through the years. As we continue on this new part of our journey, I ask that...

_____

_____

_____

_____

_____

_____

Live so that when your children think of fairness and integrity, they think of you.

H. JACKSON BROWN, JR.

Dear God, it's a beautiful and frightening process as children begin to spread their wings and discover their unique gifts and talents. I pray that You would guide my child…

_____

_____

_____

_____

_____

_____

_____

Lord, as my child begins to make choices independently, please help him or her to…

_____

_____

_____

_____

_____

_____

_____

Children have more need of models than of critics.
JOSEPH JOUBERT

Lord, as my child makes decisions that will chart a course for his or her future, I ask that...

_____
_____
_____
_____
_____
_____
_____

Dear Lord, please make Your presence known in my child's life by...

_____
_____
_____
_____
_____
_____
_____
_____

There is always a moment in childhood when the door opens and lets the future in.
GRAHAM GREENE

begin

Is it that time already? I'm not sure that I am prepared for the role of being a cheerleader from the sidelines from now on.

Please give me the assurance that the seeds I sowed into this life will bear much fruit. Help me to not worry, but to trust instead. I ask for the wisdom to know when to offer my help, when to be comforting, and when to be firm.

You have done a good work, Father, in my child. Through all the ups and downs, You have brought us to this good time and place. The lines that have fallen for us are pleasant and secure.

I ask that my child will make You proud. Please bring back to my child's mind all that You directed me to instill. I ask that You will make crooked paths straight, dark places light, and rough places smooth.

As hard as this is to ask, I pray that You will never give my child so much that there would be the temptation to turn from You, or so little evil would entice. Give this child just enough to stay dependent on You and find contentment wherever You lead. Please teach my child that life does not consist of the abundance of possessions but in the knowledge of You.

As we begin this phase of our journey, may we be ever mindful that someday we will meet on that shore forever to be with You. Help us to spend each day conscious of that.

More love than ever,

Dear Lord, as my child begins life on his or her own, please…

_____

_____

_____

_____

_____

_____

_____

God, as I consider where my child's relationship
with You is at, I pray…

_____

_____

_____

_____

_____

_____

There are only two lasting bequests we can hope to give our children.
One of these is roots, the other, wings.
HODDING CARTER

*T*errible blunders will be made—disappointments and failures, hurts and losses of every kind. And they'll keep making them even after they've found themselves too, of course, because growing up is a process that goes on and on. And every hard knock they ever get, knocks the father even harder still, if that's possible, and if and when they finally come through more or less in one piece at the end, there's maybe no rejoicing greater than his in all creation.

FREDERIC BUECHNER

*S*hortly after my son and daughter were born, I started praying for their respective wife and husband. I'm still praying, and will be until they are married…Some may think these prayers are premature. They are not. Next to their decision to receive Jesus, marriage is the most important decision our children will ever make. It will affect the rest of their lives, not to mention the lives of other family members…And since only God knows who will make the best marriage partner for anyone, He should be consulted first and He should give the final answer.

STORMIE OMARTIAN
The Power of a Praying® Parent

Father, please help me to be a voice of wisdom and a continuing positive influence on my child even as my child makes his or her own way. My prayer is that…

_____

_____

_____

_____

_____

_____

_____

_____

_____

_____

Give me the life of the boy whose mother is nurse, seamstress, washerwoman, cook, teacher, angel, and saint, all in one, and whose father is guide, exemplar, and friend. No servants to come between. These are the boys who are born to the best fortune.

ANDREW CARNEGIE

A **child** enters your home and for the next **twenty** **years** makes so much **noise** you can hardly stand it. The child departs, **leaving** the house so **silent** you think you are going mad.

— John Andrew Holmes

37

Dear Lord, as I consider my child's future, my most fervent prayer is…

_____

_____

_____

_____

_____

_____

_____

38

Lord, it's so new and strange to become more like a peer than a parent to my child. Please bless our relationship with…

_____

_____

_____

_____

_____

_____

_____

Children's children are a crown to the aged, and parents are the pride of their children.
THE BOOK OF PROVERBS

Life

A PARENT'S PRAYER ON SALVATION

MY FATHER GOD, The day salvation was offered to me was the day my life truly began. The gratitude I feel that I am now Your child, destined for eternity with You in heaven, is more than I can put into mere words. Not only have You granted me salvation through Jesus, but You have extended that to my family. There is no better thought than to know we will live as a family together with You in heaven. It's a day I look forward to and live with the knowledge that no force on earth or hell can change that.

May every word and deed reflect that I am a new creation based only on the redemption I have received from You. Help me, Father, to be a living example of You to my family. Let me not ever be tempted to turn away from You or take my eyes off the Savior who died for me. I ask for Your help, both for my loved ones and me, that our lives may reflect You. Hold us, dear Father, in the palms of Your hands, where nothing can upset or distract us from Your plan. Guide us by Your Holy Spirit through this life.

Please accept my life, our lives, as a reciprocal act of Your having chosen us first.

With all my love,

_____

A CHILD'S PRAYER OF SALVATION

LORD JESUS, I ask You to come into my heart to live forever. I invite You into my life as my Lord and Savior. You died for me, and now I want to live for You. Please help me so that the things I hear, the friends I have, or the things I see will never draw me away from You. Please forgive me of my sins and help me to follow You all the days of my life.
I love You, Jesus,

_____

Lord, as I consider my child's spiritual needs,
I ask You that…

_____

_____

_____

_____

_____

_____

_____

_____

_____

_____

_____

_____

42

*A*cknowledge and take to heart this day that the LORD
is God in heaven above and on the earth below. There is no other.
Keep his decrees and commands, which I am giving you today, so that
it may go well with you and your children after you and that you may
live long in the land the LORD your God gives you for all time.

THE BOOK OF DEUTERONOMY

Dear Lord, please help me to see all that You are doing in the spiritual life of my child. Please show me…

_____
_____
_____
_____
_____
_____
_____

Father God, as my child learns more about Your life and Your love, I ask that You show my child…

_____
_____
_____
_____
_____
_____
_____

*The Lord says, "As surely as I live, your children will be like jewels.
You will be as proud of them as a bride is of her jewels."*

THE BOOK OF ISAIAH (NCV)

Hear, O children, the instruction
    of a parent,
And give attention that you may
    gain understanding,
For I give you sound teaching;
Do not abandon my instruction.
Acquire wisdom!
    Acquire understanding!
Do not forget nor turn away
    from the words of my mouth.
Do not forsake her,
    and she will guard you;
Love her, and she will watch over you.
I have directed you in the way
    of wisdom;
I have led you in upright paths.
When you walk, your steps
    will not be impeded;
And if you run, you will not stumble.
Take hold of instruction; do not let go.
Guard her, for she is your life.

The Book of Proverbs (NCV)

Dear God, as I turn over my child's life to You, my prayer is that…

_____

_____

_____

_____

_____

_____

_____

_____

_____

As a **father** has **compassion** on his children, so the LORD has **compassion** on those who **fear him**.

The Book of Psalms

*C*ome, my children,
listen to me; I will teach you
the fear of the LORD.
Whoever of you loves life and
desires to see many good days, keep
your tongue from evil and your
lips from speaking lies.
Turn from evil and do good;
seek peace and pursue it.

The Book of Psalms